Will
I
Think
of
You?

Leonard
Nimoy

with Photographs by Mr. Nimoy

Celestial Arts
Millbrae, Ca 94030

To Sandi

Copyright ©1974 by Celestial Arts
231 Adrian Road, Millbrae, California 94030

First Printing, August 1974

Made in the United States of America

Library of Congress Cataloging in Publication Data

Nimoy, Leonard.
   Will I think of you?

   Poems.
   I. Title
PS3564.I5W5   811'.5'4   74-8357
ISBN 0-912310-70-7

   5 6 7 8 — 81 80 79 78

I.
Daybreak
and
Darkness

Will I Think Of You?

Only at sunrise
  Which is God's beginning

For you were there
  At the beginning of me

When I came alive
  And discovered my place

My worth
  The beauty of earth

And the miracle of daybreak
  Once again

And the richness of mornings
  To come

Only In The Morning

Each time
  The darkness of past
Is chased
  By the light of now

        Will I think of you . . . .

          Only then

Only at night
        Where the silence

And the blackness
        is touched occasionally
By a lonely cat
        Or suspicious puppy

A passing plane
        red eye winking
To the stars
        Who refuse to be seduced

        When I hear
                Your whispered love
        in the tree rustle

When I feel your secret hand
        exploring me
                drifting across my skin
To rest in a friendly
        harbor

        And my mind tells me
                I am alone

        But my heart knows better

        Only then

                will I think

                        Of you

II.
Seasons

Will I Think Of You?

Only when it snows

            And the whiteness
            the pure
                    virgin
                        whiteness

Covers the face
            of the earth
            To cleanse the trampled
                    corruption
                        Of times past

Like a new love
            delicate

Untracked
            Unexplored

        Waiting for the lovers
            To choose carefully
            The path to heaven
                Together

When I am overcome by
The realization that you
created the whiteness and the
                        purity

And you led me
    Like a child
            both of us children

Into
    A new and pure

    Wonderful land of our own

Where each step
    Left a priceless
            landmark

And promised a new
Place to explore
A new step to come

Then I will
    Watch the snow
  falling in swirls and flurries
  Of perfect crystal tears

I will watch
The new virginity
     embrace the earth

         And I will think of you

Only when it rains

I will recall
 An aching soul
 and a crying heart
 standing in pools
 of the saddest light

Back to back
 And moving away
And I knew
 the tears in your heart
Would soon be on your cheeks

 To wet my fingers
 As I held your face
 Up to the light
 To remember
 For tomorrow

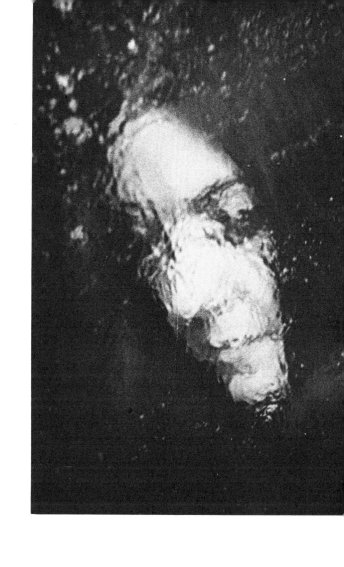

Then . . . .

Whenever the eyes of heaven
Overflow
And God's tears
Wash across
My window
I shall see again
Those streaks of love
Which flowed for me
To bind
An aching soul
To a crying heart

And I will think of you

And when the day is clear

After a rain
And a new vision
Of the landscape
Is visible to all
Who will
Bother to look
And see

When I remember how I felt
Safe enough
With you
To let you
See me

Cry

When the tears
         washed clean
The windows of my vision
And I could see
         The past and present of
Myself

   And find hope and strength
For the future

And after the rain of my crying
I felt washed

    And fresh and loved
    As my babyself
    Must have felt

When my mother
    bathed her infant

Then after each rain
    How
        Can I help
            But think of you

Will I think of you?

   Only when it's cold
And I'm shivering
      Against the wind

And suddenly from inside
      The core of me
         From my deepest depths
Comes
      A small warming flame
Which wants to grow
And I fight it
      Until I realize I need it

Want it
      To flow through me

To fill me
      Because
         It is you

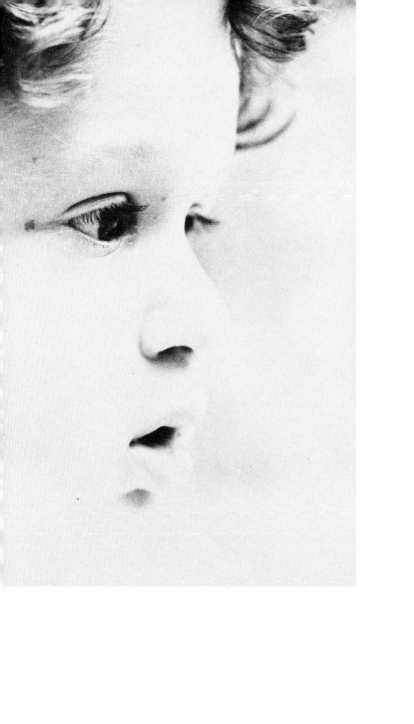

Only In The Spring

When the first warm breezes of April
Give courage
    To the youngest
        tenderest
Shoots of nature
      to appear
      to live
        to grow

When the thaw
            in the mountains
Sends the pure cold
                 Cascading
                   waters
Down the
       hillside
            To fill the streams

As you fill me
          To laughter
          And tears

               Only then . . .

                 Will I think of you

III.
Joys
and
Sorrows

Will I think of you?

Only when I feel
warmed and wanted

Though once
I felt I was outside
looking in
disconnected
Watching the world
go by

then . . . .

I'll remember
  That in your love
  I found acceptance

And I'll think of you

Only when I laugh

At a joke of others
or my own

Or a memory of you

And the laughter rises
Out of the well of me

To be tasted
By my mouth and lips

When the tickle rolls
through my body

To remind me
Of days and nights
Of free laughter with you

Even while others stared
At the crazy couple
    wondering what could be so funny
In a world
  Of grim
      rushing
           and painful
                waiting
Urgent hoping
   And sad silences

Then
    When the laughter
Is multiplied
    By past joys remembered
And I can't stop
Even to catch my breath
    Or to give relief to my aching sides

        I'll realize
            That the laughter in my life
Is for you,
        because of you

And I'll think of you

            But only then

Or when I'm sad
            and lost
    Tired of trying

When the tears and pains
        Of the world
All seem to be mine

When there is no one but you
Who would really understand
The emptiness of my soul
            The sorrow
Of trying
        And failing

            Of knowing that
    Life can be a trial

Where the judge and jury
Sometimes sit
With faces of stone
And will not respond
Even to a cry
From the truest heart

When I know
That the final precious blossom
Clinging to the tree
Will surely fall
Under the constant
Persistent
Pressing of the wind

When I know that you
And only you
  Could see all this
  And hear all this
And be with me
  In my sadness
In silent understanding

And shed tears
  for my sorrow

Then

   I will think of you

Only when the turn of fortune
Comes my way again

When I ride
The crest of triumph
glowing with pride
In the promise fulfilled

When the adoring crowd
has returned
With shouts of approval

Then I will search
Their faces
Looking for the one
Who stood beside me
In defeat
And should be there
In the victory
Which is empty
Without you

IV.
In Places

Will I think of you?

No . . . .

Only when I'm with others.

Surrounded
In a crowded
party room

Listening to
Several conversations

People communicating
Or trying to . . .

Watching the
Blur of figures and
Faces go past
none coming into focus

Except yours

Again and again
In each corner
In each chair
In every smile

Only you
persistent
forever

Only then

Will I think of you?

Only on the highway

When I travel

Searching for money and fame

And finding that neither feeds me

When I pass
  The other travelers
    Some going my way
    And some not

But I realize
That this
Is what we all
Must do . . .

To fall behind
The travelling flow
And catch up
And pass others
Then fall behind again
Passed by those
Who rush on
Believing that
It is best
To be there first

But I know that this is
Where we all are

On the highway

That there is no "here" or "there" . . . .
   There is only
     The coming and going

If we can help
One
Who finds the way
Too hard or too long
   Then that is worth
    All of being
And I will try to help

    Because someone helped me

Someone who cared more
About the brothers on the
Road
   Than about the
      Gifts at the end
And that someone was you

        So I will think of you

Only on the beach
  Where the timeless
    Never ending surge
Of water
    Changes
The face of earth
    Again and again
Each minute of the day
                    night
                    and always

  Where the children
  And the aged
  Come together
  To chase a wave
  The surf
  Or a dream

Where the tide shifts constantly
Teaching me
That today is only today
And whatever I have
Good or bad
Much or little
Must change
Or it will rot
and die

Then and there when I recall
The change
  In this thing called me
The new sides
  New forms
    New shapes of me

Which came
  When you
  Washed across
My being

Then, there
    On the beach
        I will think

        Of you

V.
At Times

I love you
I Love You
I love you
I LOVE YOU
I Love You
I LOVE YOU
I love you
I love you
I love you
I love you
I Love You
I love you
I love You

Will I Think Of You?

Only when I'm alone

Staring out my window

Into space . . .

       Which becomes you

Your love
Smiling back
   To the warmth
    Of my heart

Filling the emptiness
      The loneliness
         With your being

Only then,

    Will I think of you

Only when I hear music

    And the songs
    Of the poet singers
        remind me
That
        all things are for all
                people

    That there is
A love and a sorrow
  A joy and a pain
Which each of us separately
Feels
    As if it is ours alone

And it is only ours
Even while it is everyone's

For each of us is
A separate miracle
In a collective miracle

Brought together
For a moment
By a group of notes
And a scan of words

From the heart
Of one
Who dares
To think

That others
Might feel
As he feels

And he sings it out to us
　　as a gift

To be accepted
　　　　Or rejected

　　　　　　But given with
　　　　　　　A heart of love

I thank them
　　　the poet singers

Who give us communion

And help us join with
　　Each other
　　　　　　think of each other

And bless us
　　With each other's love

　　　　For in that music—love—rhythm

　　　　　I feel your
　　　　　　Heart beat

　　　　And I will think of you

Will I think of you?

Only when we're apart

And the aching joy-pain of our love

Surrounds me
    Filling the air I breathe

Only with each blink of my
Eye which yearns
To re-open to find you here
With me

Only with
Each clock-tick
Which makes my ear perk up
Hopeful
That it has heard
Your key in the door

Only when I day dream and
re-dream
Our coming together again

When the world will fall away
leaving only two figures

Yours and mine

Merged into
A classic cord

Loving . . .

Being loved
In each
part of harmony

Only
When I die

And realize
That I am born again

For dying is

A beginning

And I
have died
thousands of times

Sometimes
Several times a day

I am learning
That from each death
　　Comes a new vision
Of life

　　A new sense of the miracle
　　Of being and creation

For fear
　　Is worse than dying . . .

Fear prevents discovery
　　And destroys the creative flow
　　Of God-man's soul

And when I let my old self
Hardened and rigid
Die

I am re-born
Vital, open and fresh

And this discovery
This victory over the
Fear of death
Came

When I thought I was dead
And found you

So
Each time
I rise
Out of the ashes
Of my fear
I will gratefully

Think of you

Only on Special Days

Birthdays, Holidays

And other days . . . .

When those who
    Give to each other
        And live for each other

        Travel
            For hours or days
                Or for an instant

    To hold
        Or dream-hold
  Each other

To exchange
    Heart-warmth
      And body-warmth

When we commemorate

And Celebrate

The Special days
Of a life of love

Then and especially then

Because the day is special
As your glorious being
Is special

I will think of you

Only when we're together

And I can think of nothing else

And everything else

Because we together

Are everything

And our togetherness is

All things

Then as always

And forever

I will think of you